BRICK FLICKS

BRICK FLICKS

60 CULT MOVIE SCENES AND POSTERS MADE FROM LEGO®

WARREN ELSMORE

MITCHELL
BEAZLEY

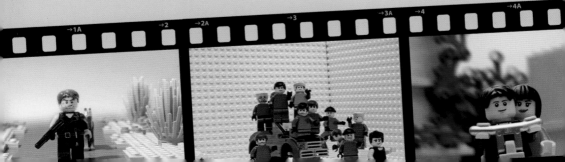

Brick Flicks
by Warren Elsmore

First published in Great Britain in 2014 by Mitchell Beazley, an imprint of Octopus Publishing Group Limited,
Endeavour House, 189 Shaftesbury Avenue, London WC2H 8JY
www.octopusbooks.co.uk

An Hachette UK Company
www.hachette.co.uk

The publishers will be grateful for any information that will assist them in keeping future
editions up to date. Although all reasonable care has been taken in the preparation of
this book, neither the publishers nor the author can accept any liability for any consequence
arising from the use thereof, or the information contained therein.

The author has asserted his moral rights.

A CIP record for this book is available from the British Library.
ISBN 978-1-84533-975-3
QTT.LEGM

This book was conceived, designed and produced by
Quintet Publishing Limited
114–116 Western Road
Hove, East Sussex
BN3 1DD
United Kingdom

Photographer: Michael Wolchover (unless otherwise stated)
Text: Ian Haydn Smith
Designer: Gareth Butterworth
Art Director: Michael Charles
Project Editor: Caroline Elliker
Editorial Assistants: Ella Lines, Alice Sambrook
Editorial Director: Emma Bastow
Publisher: Mark Searle

10 9 8 7 6 5 4 3 2 1

Printed in China by Toppan Leefung

CONTENTS

INTRODUCTION

There are perhaps few toys as iconic as LEGO® bricks. However, in the 55 years since the LEGO brick was born, another industry has created thousands of iconic images that we've grown to know and love. What better way to celebrate the motion picture industry than by recreating these images in LEGO form?

In *Brick Flicks* we've recreated 60 famous movies from one of the earliest colour films, *The Wizard of Oz* (1939), right up to the computer-generated imagery of *The Life of Pi* (2012). Our journey takes us through action, comedy, drama, science fiction and more as we celebrate the versatility of the LEGO palette. Each film brings its own challenges as we strive to create an instantly recognisable image.

As with most big screen productions, many of our *Brick Flicks* use iconic characters to further the story. To make sure that I could do justice to these characters, I've had the pleasure of working with the amazing team at Minifigs.me once again. Caroline and Nick Savage first worked with me on *Brick City* to create the wonderful British Royal Family image. In *Brick Flicks* I challenged them to create a whole cast of characters and I'm sure you'll agree that they have produced some fantastic custom minifigures to complement our backdrops and lighting. The next challenge is to photograph the scene, and shooting LEGO elements well is a real skill. I'm lucky enough to work with a fantastic photographer in my studio who knows how to handle the highly reflective bricks. Finally, while we've tried to keep the images as true to life as possible, the final step in some cases is on the computer. Shooting at such a tiny scale means that our depth of field (the amount of image in focus) is tiny! This necessitates merging multiple images to create the final shot.

With the release of *The LEGO Movie* in 2014, the worlds of the silver screen and the plastic brick have been brought closer together than ever before. As with our book though, recreating LEGO bricks on film was only half the challenge. LEGO models have a certain tongue-in-cheek charm about them that is part of the essence of a toy. While recreating my favourite movie scenes, I've tried to keep that same humour running throughout. The terrifying movie poster from *Jaws*, for instance, is that little less frightening when the shark is a LEGO element!

Within *The LEGO Movie*, the hero Emmet must learn to use the bricks he has on hand to build without instructions. Only by learning to do this can Emmet become a true 'Master Builder'. In *Brick Flicks* we've given you the same challenge. While some of our films come with instructions to build a film prop – most of them do not, they rely on simple ingenuity and imagination. So if I haven't included your favourite film, why not try to use your imagination and create your own Brick Flick?

I hope you enjoy looking through *Brick Flicks* as much as we've enjoyed creating the images, and if your favourite film is here, I hope we've done your memories justice!

Warren Elsmore

CUSTOMISED MINIFIGS

Every so often, a contract comes through the doors of Minifigs.me that makes us grin from ear to ear. *Brick Flicks* was one of those – an opportunity for us to put our experience to work in recreating some truly iconic film stars as custom LEGO® minifigures.

Each one has been made with extreme care and attention to detail. We start with a reference photo – a classic scene from *Singin' in the Rain*, or perhaps the confident stance of *Citizen Kane*. Studying each character carefully, we try to pick out the quirks and features that make them unique. It could be a tuft of straw coming from the jacket of the Scarecrow in *The Wizard of Oz* or the beguiling, charismatic smile of Holly Golightly in *Breakfast at Tiffany's*. We've found if you can capture those details, the figure comes to life with a charm all of its own. You can work for hours on the sharp suit, but it's the little human quirks that give a figure its soul.

After we've got the design, it's a case of carefully selecting just the right parts to do the minifig justice. Once we have the blank figure ready, we feed it into our super high-tech printer. The final result is something very special – whether it's a film star for *Brick Flicks* or a bespoke minifig for a customer. With all the time and care that's been devoted to the creation of *Brick Flicks*, we're extremely proud to have been a part of this collaboration.

Caroline and Nick Savage, Minifigs.me

2001: A SPACE ODYSSEY

Director: Stanley Kubrick

Year: 1968

Starring: Keir Dullea, Gary Lockwood, William Sylvester, Daniel Richter, Leonard Rossiter

Few films can equal the vision of Stanley Kubrick's magnificent 1968 opus. A black obelisk appears throughout history, from the dawn of Man to the near and distant future. It may have some impact on the way our species was created or developed. It may even hold the key to the meaning of our existence. Not that Kubrick and his co-screenwriter, science fiction novelist Arthur C. Clarke, were ever going to tell us. Clarke once famously said, 'If you understand 2001 completely, we failed. We want to raise far more questions than we answered.' But that's not all the film does. From the celebrated scenes of a space station spinning around the Earth and the descent to the moon, both set to Johann Strauss II's 'The Blue Danube' waltz, to the dazzling 'Star Gate' sequence, underpinned by the music of György Ligeti, the true wonder of Kubrick's achievement is that he visualises these worlds with exacting precision, before any actual spacecraft had ever left the Earth's orbit, let alone landed on the moon. Certain décor aside, the film has dated little and remains far more convincing than subsequent space films, including recent Oscar winner, *Gravity* (2013).

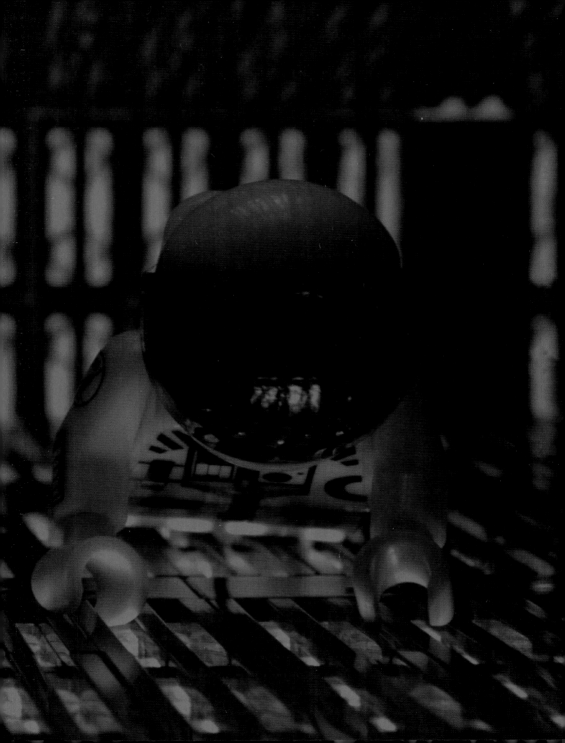

ALIEN

Director: Ridley Scott

Year: 1979

Starring: Sigourney Weaver, John Hurt, Tom Skerritt, Ian Holm, Harry Dean Stanton, Veronica Cartwright, Yaphet Koto

Ridley Scott's career-defining second film is the perfect blend of genres. It takes the stalker horror film and sets it in outer space. 'The Texas Chainsaw Massacre of science fiction', as the director described it. The crew of the spaceship Nostromo is awakened from deep sleep by an SOS signal from a nearby planet. On landing, one of the crew is attacked by an alien creature that attaches itself to his face. Returned to the main ship, the man seems to recover before dying violently in front of his colleagues, whose lives are threatened by this deadly creature. Cue a thrilling and terrifying journey into the belly of this great ship, as the crew attempt to destroy the beast, only to find themselves picked off by it, one by one. Its clichéd script notwithstanding, Alien is a magnificent, space-set Grand Guignol, with stunning designs by artist H. R. Geiger and a series of memorable set pieces, including the now famous scene where John Hurt becomes the first victim of the alien creature.

1x   1x   1x   4x   3x

ALIEN

The second appearance by the alien, after it is removed from Kane's face, unfolds after the crew member has come out of a coma and is enjoying a meal. Appearing to choke on some food, he soon collapses and his body spasms before an alien bursts out of his stomach. Ridley Scott had chosen not to inform the cast that blood would spray everywhere, and the shock on their faces is very real. The small alien scurries off to a dark recess of the ship, where it transforms into the mighty, seemingly indestructible creature that hunts down the crew.

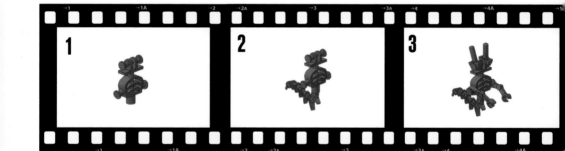

BLADE RUNNER

Director: Ridley Scott

Year: 1982

Starring: Harrison Ford, Rutger Hauer, Sean Young, Daryl Hannah, William Sanderson, Joe Turkel, Brion James

Few films can claim to be as influential as Ridley Scott's loose adaptation of Philip K. Dick's *Only Androids Dream of Electric Sheep*. It opens in Los Angeles, in 2019. Six androids have escaped from an off-world colony and illegally returned to Earth. Deckard, an ex-Blade Runner, a cop that specialises in hunting down rogue droids, is charged with 'retiring' them. His hunt leads him to Tyrrel, the head of the corporation that created the droids and from whom they seek the ultimate prize: to prolong their existence. Unlike most earlier science fiction films, the world in *Blade Runner* is portrayed as a grungy, 'retro-fitted' and chaotic place. Scott films it with a sparse and atmospheric use of lighting, a style that would come to define his subsequent work.

CLOSE ENCOUNTERS OF THE THIRD KIND

Director: Steven Spielberg

Year: 1977

Starring: Richard Dreyfus, Teri Garr, Melinda Dillon, François Truffaut, Bob Balaban

Steven Spielberg's account of mankind's first major encounter with aliens portrays them as a benevolent species. Richard Dreyfus plays Roy Neary who, late one night, encounters an alien light. Like many others who saw it, he is drawn to Devil's Tower in Wyoming, where the most incredible events then take place. The story was inspired by a meteor shower Spielberg watched with his father, and his first version of the film was the amateur feature *Firelight*, which he wrote when he was just 16. *Close Encounters* unfolds on a grander scale, but the story remains simple, much like the five-note piece of music that John Williams composed as the mode of communication between humanity and the alien mothership, whose coloured lights transform the film's climax into a euphoric phantasmagoria.

DRACULA

Director: Tod Browning

Year: 1931

Starring: Bela Lugosi, Helen Chandler, David Manners, Dwight Frye, Edward Van Sloan

Although F. W. Murnau's classic *Nosferatu* (1922) was the first film inspired by Bram Stoker's novel, Todd Browning's Hollywood production was the first adaptation sanctioned by the author's widow. Renfield, an estate agent, travels to Count Dracula's castle in Transylvania to seal an agreement that gives the count ownership of Carfax Abbey in England. He returns home by ship, but it docks with everyone on board dead, except for an insane Renfield, and with an empty coffin in the cargo hold. Ashore, Dracula mixes with London's high society and encounters Mina and her fiancée Jonathan Harker. She is the embodiment of Dracula's desires and will ultimately be his undoing. When the silent horror movie star Lon Chaney became too ill to play the Count, Universal Studios looked at a host of actors before deciding on the relatively cheap Bela Lugosi, who had played Dracula on Broadway a decade earlier and whose image would define the character for decades to come. The film was a huge success and helped to forge the studio's reputation as the home of horror during the 1930s.

E.T.
THE EXTRA-
TERRESTRIAL

Director: Steven Spielberg

Year: 1982

Starring: Henry Thomas, Drew Barrymore, Dee Wallace, Peter Coyote

A modern-day fairy tale, a thrilling adventure, and quite possibly one of the greatest science fiction films ever made, Steven Spielberg's seventh feature was the biggest box office success of the 1980s. It tells the story of a small alien trapped on Earth when its spaceship departs the planet, inadvertently leaving it here. E.T. befriends Elliott, a young boy, who gathers his friends and, with the help of his younger sister, finds a way to evade the authorities and help E.T. make his way back home. Drawing on his own childhood experience of having an imaginary friend following the divorce of his parents, Spielberg's film is ultimately a celebration of innocence. This is a child's view of the world, and for the first half, with the exception of Dee Wallace's mother, we never see above the waist of any adult. To draw out child stars Henry Thomas and Drew Barrymore's emotional responses, Spielberg shot most of the film sequentially. And to humanise his alien, E.T.'s features were inspired by the faces of American writers Carl Sandburg and Ernest Hemingway, and the scientist Albert Einstein.

21

ELLIOTT'S BIKE

We all dream at some point of being able to fly. It's no surprise that Elliott's trip into the skies is one of the film's most memorable moments, aided in no small part by John Williams' score, which won him his fourth Oscar and second for a Spielberg film. Elliott takes E.T. for a bike ride, but before long the small alien is controlling the journey, which finds them heading towards a precipice, only for the bike to launch into the sky and, in one magical shot, glide across the face of the moon.

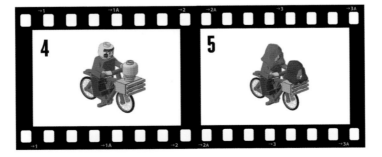

MAD MAX 2: THE ROAD WARRIOR

Director: George Miller

Year: 1981

Starring: Mel Gibson, Bruce Spence, Vernon Wells, Michael Preston, Virginia Hey

One of the best examples of a sequel outdoing the original, George Miller's stark, post-apocalyptic demolition derby features Mel Gibson as Max, a battle-scarred anti-hero who, with his mangy dog, searches for petrol, food and water from the many wrecked vehicles along an abandoned highway in the Australian outback. By chance, he encounters a community besieged by a group of savages hell-bent on destroying them and taking their seemingly unlimited oil resources. Before long, the two groups go to battle on the open road, with Max at the heart of the action. Miller expands on the first film's simple premise by creating a mythic hero for the times. Mel Gibson, whose star was still on the rise, is captivating, striking a balance between rebellion and heroism. And the final, epic vehicular mash-up, whose carnage resulted in numerous injuries for the film's stunt team, has rarely been topped.

JAWS

Director: Steven Spielberg

Year: 1975

Starring: Roy Scheider, Richard Dreyfus, Robert Shaw, Lorraine Gary, Murray Hamilton

Jaws unfolds in the fictional resort of Amity, where the town's police chief, Brody, finds the dismembered body of a young woman and is worried it might be a shark attack. When a small boy is the next victim, he journeys out to sea with Richard Dreyfus's oceanographer and Robert Shaw's crusty fisherman to capture the beast. Their optimism soon vanishes when they see the size of the shark, whose dismantling of their vessel results in a brutal fight for survival. Has any film ever affected our psyche so much? Going to the beach today is certainly different from the time before *Jaws* was released. Never mind the fact that the shark, when we finally see it out of water, hardly looks real. Spielberg's white-knuckle journey into the mouth of the beast is a worthy cinematic successor to *Moby Dick*, and ushered in the modern blockbuster. More than that, with his montage of tourists arriving for their summer holidays and fantastic dialogue that fine-tunes the nuances of the characters, both major and minor, Spielberg created a richly textured thrill-ride that announced the arrival of Hollywood's most successful filmmaker.

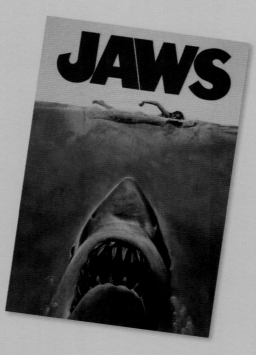

FLASH GORDON

Director: Mike Hodges

Year: 1980

Starring: Sam Jones, Melody Anderson, Max Von Sydow, Topol, Ornella Muti, Timothy Dalton, Brian Blessed, Peter Wyngarde

Space goes camp in Mike Hodges' gleefully outré update of the 1930s comic serial. When Earth is subjected to a series of catastrophic natural disasters, only the 'mad' scientist Dr Hans Zarkov believes it to be the work of an alien force. Taking football star Flash Gordon and reporter Dale Arden hostage, he travels to the planet Mongo to face the Emperor of the Universe, Ming the Merciless, to find a way to save their planet. With a series of bizarre performances by the likes of Ornella Muti, Timothy Dalton and acclaimed British playwright John Osborne, *Flash Gordon* profits from never taking itself too seriously. Nowhere is this more apparent than in Max Von Sydow's wonderfully arch take on Ming, a far more interesting character than Sam Jones's dull frat-boy hero. (Jones reprised his role for Seth MacFarlane's 2012 comedy *Ted*.) Imaginative set-design allows different planets their own colour-coded décor and everything is scored to the pulsating music of Queen, whose over-the-top theme song pretty much sums up the experience you'll get watching this deliriously entertaining film.

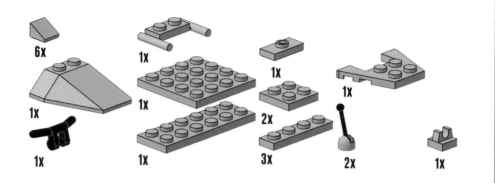

6x

1x

1x

1x

1x

1x

1x

2x

3x

1x

2x

1x

FLASH GORDON

One of the most thrilling scenes in *Flash Gordon* is the hero's escape from Sky City, which faces imminent destruction after Klytus, Ming's second-in-command, is killed. Finding a rocket cycle, Flash launches the craft from an escape chute moments before the floating metropolis explodes. Summoning his allies, he then leads an attack on Mingo City, hopefully in time to stop the evil emperor from marrying Dale Arden and the Earth from being destroyed, in that order.

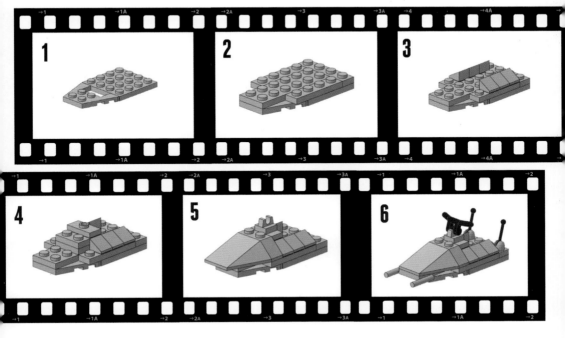

PLANET OF THE APES

Director: Franklin J. Schaffner

Year: 1968

Starring: Charlton Heston, Roddy McDowell, Kim Hunter, Maurice Evans, James Whitmore

A spacecraft lands on a strange planet where evolution has seen apes move to the top of the food chain, and the species of human that exists there is little more than an incommunicative, feral creature. After a gorilla shoots his colleague and he sees how humans are treated, surviving astronaut Taylor decides to organise a revolt with the help of some sympathetic apes. Franklin J. Schaffner's adaptation of the French novel by Pierre Boulle, whose wartime experiences were the source for *The Bridge on the River Kwai*, filmed by David Lean in 1957, is a stark and brutal drama, capturing the anarchic spirit of a changing culture in 1960s America. The narrative can be seen as an allegory of racism, or a call to arms against an oppressive and authoritarian government. It is also a thrilling sci-fi movie with a stunning twist. John Chambers won an Oscar for outstanding make-up achievement, in the same year that *2001: A Space Odyssey* was released. There is a suggestion that many people believed the actors playing apes at the beginning of Kubrick's film were in fact real apes.

PSYCHO

Director: Alfred Hitchcock

Year: 1960

Starring: Janet Leigh, Anthony Perkins, Vera Miles, John Gavin

Alfred Hitchcock's relatively low-budget horror film was a risk for the Hollywood director. Shocking by the standards of the times, it could have sunk his career. Without giving one of cinema's great twists away, it follows Marion Crane, who steals money from her work and, after leaving town in a hurry, stops for the night at a deserted motel. There, she encounters the owner, Norman Bates, who is not at all what he seems. Marion takes a shower and audiences watched one of the biggest cinematic shocks of the era. Hitchcock, developing a marketing strategy that was unique at the time, stipulated that no one be permitted to enter the cinema after the film had started, and requested that audiences not reveal any of the plot to those who had yet to see the film. Hitchcock's faith in the project saw him invest personally in it. Unlike the films he made that bookend *Psycho*, the film was made on the cheap and in black and white, with crew members from his *Alfred Hitchcock Presents* TV series. It paid off in the end. *Psycho* was a success with audiences and it now ranks as one of the finest horror movies ever made.

THE BIRDS

Director: Alfred Hitchcock

Year: 1963

Starring: Tippi Hedren, Rod Taylor, Jessica Tandy, Suzanne Pleshette

Pushing the boundaries of what he could show on the screen, even more than *Psycho* (1960), Hitchcock's startling adaptation of Daphne Du Maurier's novella was the third and final of his films based on her work (after 1939's misguided attempt to film *Jamaica Inn* and a far superior version of *Rebecca* [1940], his first Hollywood film) and, for many, his last great masterpiece. Tippi Hedren made her big-screen debut as Melanie Daniels who, following an encounter with Rod Taylor's charming stranger, visits him at his home in the sleepy coastal town of Bodega Bay. No sooner has she arrived than a series of attacks involving birds plague the town. As they increase in their ferocity, some townsfolk believe Melanie is to blame. Hitchcock's film is a mystery with no solution. Amidst the carnage of the birds' attacks, we never quite understand why these events are happening, which only increases our fascination with what we see. An experimental soundtrack was used for the film, which intended to replicate bird sounds rather than rely on a conventional score to underpin the action. And state-of-the-art special effects were blended with footage of real birds. Not for the faint of heart.

MEN IN BLACK

Director: Barry Sonnenfeld

Year: 1997

Starring: Will Smith, Tommy Lee Jones, Linda Fiorentino, Vincent D'Onofrio, Rip Torn, Tony Shalhoub

Barry Sonnenfeld's take on Lowell Cunningham's comic book series is an enjoyably silly sci-fi adventure comedy that borrows as much from 1960s spy capers as it does from decades of B-movies. It follows the exploits of K, a veteran MIB agent, and rookie J, in the hunt for an alien who has taken human form and whose antics threaten the immediate future of Earth. Tommy Lee Jones's craggy, unsmiling curmudgeon is the perfect foil to Will Smith's manic new recruit, as they work their way through an alien-infested city in search of their suspect. Sonnenfeld keeps the action coming thick and fast, never allowing the tone to rise above the whimsical. Originally, the film was set in various locations across America, from Kansas to Washington DC. It was the director's idea to locate the action in New York City, believing that its citizens were used to strange behaviour and would not be perturbed by an alien disguised as a human and acting weirdly.

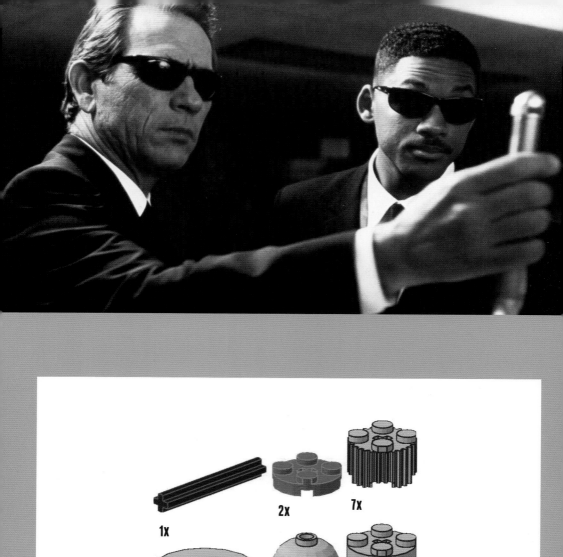

NEURALYSER

A key tool of the MIB agents is the neuralyser. When pointed at anyone not wearing a pair of the ultra-cool regulation sunglasses, the instrument renders blank a subject's short-term memory, allowing an alien encounter to be forgotten. Not dissimilar to *Doctor Who's* Sonic Screwdriver in terms of its usefulness, the neuralyser is a clever device for explaining why no one has ever uncovered the identity of this galactic agency or seen any of its extraterrestrial employees.

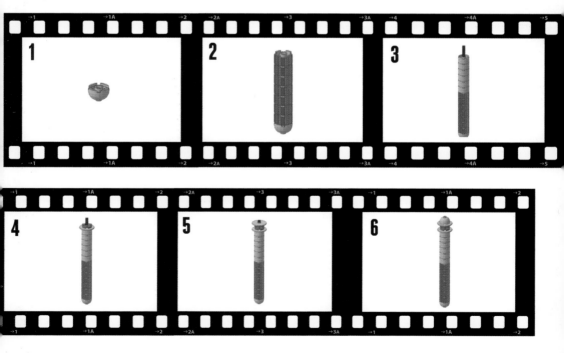

TRON

Director: Steven Lisberger

Year: 1982

Starring: Jeff Bridges, Bruce Boxleitner, David Warner, Barnard Hughes

Kevin Flynn is a computer whiz attempting to prove his old colleague stole a number of his games. However, he is unaware that the mainframe computer of the organisation he used to work for has developed an artificial intelligence that intends to take control of the world's defence systems. When Flynn tries to breach its security, the computer fires a laser at him, transporting him into the mainframe, where he becomes a participant in a series of deadly games, created by the computer to destroy any programs that still believe users exist. With its great premise, *Tron* revels in taking us inside a virtual world, a kind of deadly Olympics, where the mainframe is brutal in its punishment and hope lies in the eponymous hero, whose skills appear greater than any opponent. The film was inspired by the first widely played computer game, Pong, which was released by Atari in 1976 and involved two paddles hitting a ball back and forth, not dissimilar to table tennis. The film has attracted a cult audience over the years and a sequel, *Tron: Legacy*, was released in 2010.

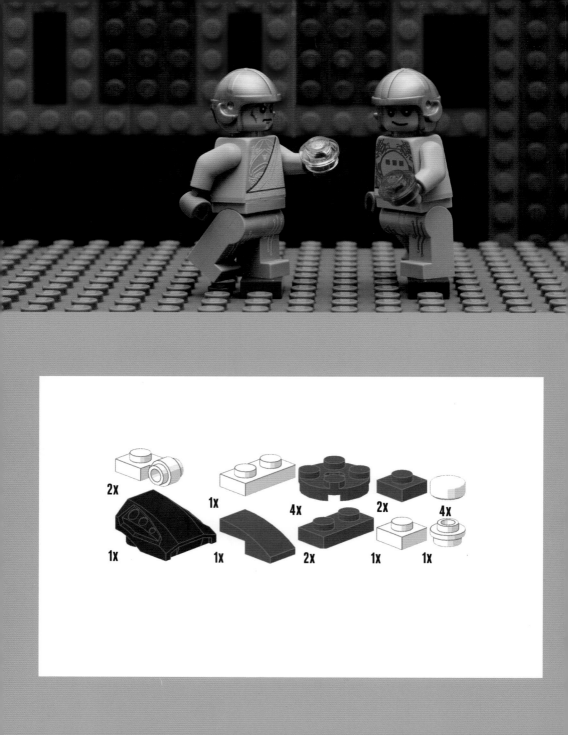

LIGHT CYCLE

Set against a digital backdrop and electronic soundtrack, *Tron's* light cycle sequence is the embodiment of 1980s style and sound. At the time, the sequence was revolutionary, thanks to the use of groundbreaking CGI technology. The 2010 remake recreates the original light cycle sequence – integral to the cult classic – during which the cycles leave a constant wall of light behind while travelling at incredibly high speeds in battle. Any opponent who crosses through another's light trail is immediately destroyed.

THE SHINING

Director: Stanley Kubrick

Year: 1980

Starring: Jack Nicholson, Shelley Duvall, Danny Lloyd, Scatman Crothers, Barry Nelson

For many, the finest horror film ever made, Stanley Kubrick's adaptation of Stephen King's novel unfolds in the eerie Overlook Hotel, where Jack Torrence arrives as caretaker for the winter, bringing with him his wife Wendy and son Danny. Within weeks, Jack's behaviour becomes erratic, until he finally goes insane and on the rampage. Robin Williams, Robert De Niro and Harrison Ford were considered for the lead role before Kubrick returned to his original choice, Jack Nicholson. All of the sets were built in England, with some location work carried out by a second unit in the US. (Outtakes for the opening shot, of the family's journey to the hotel, were used at the end of the 1982 release of *Blade Runner.*) The shoot lasted over a year, leaving Nicholson exasperated and Shelley Duvall on the verge of a breakdown. The result is a profoundly unsettling film, whose shots of murdered twin sisters, a rotting corpse coming to life, and blood cascading out of a lift are the stuff of nightmares – although not for author King, who has gone on record to say how disappointed he was with the film.

LAWRENCE OF ARABIA

Director: David Lean

Year: 1962

Starring: Peter O'Toole, Omar Sharif, Alec Guinness, Anthony Quinn, Jack Hawkins, Claude Rains, Anthony Quale, José Ferrer

For all its vast panoramas, grand battle scenes and a stirring score by Maurice Jarre, *Lawrence of Arabia* is that oddest of epics – an intimate account of one period in a fascinating man's life. T. E. Lawrence was an outspoken officer in the Signals Corps during the First World War. Ordered on an exploratory mission into the desert, he accepts and is no sooner dispatched than he finds himself drawn into the inner circle of Prince Faisal, who sees in him a like-minded spirit. Lawrence leads a union of Bedouins against the Turkish army and, as his power grows, he sees an opportunity for the Arabs to reclaim their lands. Rather than opt for a sweeping heroic account, Lean presents a complex portrait of a man driven by demons. He cast the relatively unknown Peter O'Toole in the lead, whose intensity, aided in no small part by his handsome looks and startling blue eyes, allows audiences the opportunity to understand this mercurial figure. And if you look closely at the camel he rides, you can see the rubber mat O'Toole bought to make his scenes on the beast a little less uncomfortable. The rest of the cast soon followed suit.

49

BEN-HUR

Director: William Wyler

Year: 1959

Starring: Charlton Heston, Jack Hawkins, Stephen Boyd, Haya Harareet, Martha Scott, Sam Jaffe

Winner of 11 Oscars, a record not matched until *Titanic* in 1997, William Wyler's biblical spectacle brought the Hollywood sand and sandals epic into the modern age. It tells the story of Judah Ben-Hur, a wealthy prince and merchant in Jerusalem, whose unwillingness to oppose his people and side with the occupying Roman forces sees him endure countless indignities before he finds his faith in Christ and carries out an act of charity that reunites him with his family. Though visually similar to Cecil B. DeMille's *The Ten Commandments* (1956), *Ben-Hur*'s dialogue is a great deal more contemporary. Marlon Brando, Paul Newman, Burt Lancaster and Rock Hudson were considered for the lead role, but each turned it down. Kirk Douglas expressed an interest, but Charlton Heston, no stranger to the epic, having already played Moses in DeMille's film, was eventually cast. As a result, Douglas would go on to produce and star in *Spartacus* the following year. *Ben-Hur* was one of Hollywood's most expensive productions, although all that money can be seen on the screen, from the immense sets to the action set pieces, such as the sea battle between the Romans and Macedonian pirates, and the legendary chariot race.

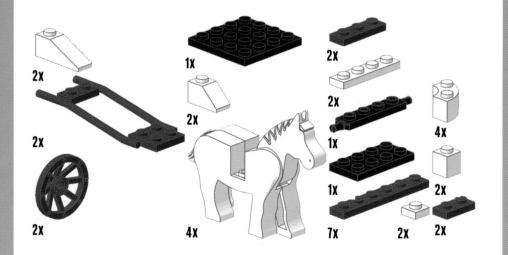

2x

1x

2x

2x

2x

2x

2x

1x

4x

4x

1x

1x

2x

7x

2x

2x

BEN-HUR

The set for the chariot race in *Ben-Hur* was the largest ever built, spanning 18 acres of land. It took over a year to complete. Both Charlton Heston and Stephen Boyd were required to learn how to ride chariots, and the sequences that made their way into the film were actually filmed by second unit directors Andrew Marton and Yakima Canutt. One of their assistant directors was Sergio Leone, who would go on to direct his own epics. It is the film's most famous scene, yet in the script it only appears as three words: 'the chariot race'.

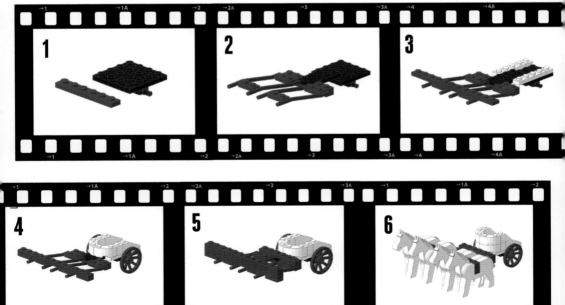

BRICKFAST AT TIFFANY'S

Director: Blake Edwards

Year: 1961

Starring: Audrey Hepburn, George Peppard, Patricia Neal, Buddy Ebsen, Mickey Rooney, Martin Balsam

Brickfast at Tiffany's tells the story of Holly Golightly, a good-time girl looking for love and wealth in equal measure, but if push came to shove, wealth would win out. When a young writer moves into her apartment building and is clearly besotted with her, Holly wonders if the course her life has taken is for the best. Author Truman Capote, who always figured Marilyn Monroe would play his creation, was incensed at the casting of Audrey Hepburn, but in the years since the film was released, the actress's look has become one of the most iconic images in fashion history. New York has rarely appeared better, the film's bittersweet tone blending with the magisterial vistas of the Manhattan skyline to create a mood of romantic longing that permeates every scene. Only Mickey Rooney, playing a cartoon version of a Japanese tenant, strikes a sour note, a casting decision that director Blake Edwards has since admitted was a mistake and a blemish on an otherwise delightful movie. As for 'Moon River', the classic song sung by Hepburn in the film, composer Henry Mancini has said he wrote it in just half an hour.

DEATH ON THE NILE

Director: John Guillermin

Year: 1978

Starring: Peter Ustinov, Mia Farrow, Bette Davis, Jane Birkin, Lois Chiles, Angela Lansbury, David Niven, Maggie Smith, Simon MacCorkindale

This is the most exotic of Agatha Christie film adaptations and, like the earlier and more cohesive *Murder on the Orient Express* (1974), it features a glittering cast of established stars, serious actors and newcomers. Topping the bill is Peter Ustinov as the Belgian detective Hercule Poirot, who was originally planning a quiet cruise down Egypt's celebrated river aboard a paddle steamer before he finds himself investigating a series of murders. Although Ustinov pitches his performance perfectly and other cast members, particularly David Niven, Mia Farrow, Lois Chiles and Simon MacCorkindale, capture the spirit of Christie's world, the real star of the film is Egypt and the stunning historical sights along the Nile. However, shooting on location was not to everyone's taste. Bette Davis, who plays the irascible Mrs Van Schuyler and was infamous for her forthrightness, commented, 'In the older days, they'd have built the Nile for you. Nowadays, the films have become travelogues and actors stuntmen.'

CASABLANCA

Director: Michael Curtiz

Year: 1942

Starring: Humphrey Bogart, Ingrid Bergman, Paul Heinreid, Claude Rains, Peter Lorre, Sidney Greenstreet, Conrad Veidt

Casablanca was made when producers and not directors held sway in Hollywood. It tells the story of Ilsa and her husband Victor, wanted by the Nazis for his work with the resistance, who arrive in Casablanca hoping to find a route out of Europe. At Rick's Café Américain, they meet its owner, with whom Ilsa had had an affair years before. With both the Nazis and Vichy French police in pursuit, Ilsa has to convince Rick that there is more to life than their love and to help her husband. The film was the brainchild of wunderkind producer Hal B. Wallis, who oversaw the numerous re-writes, chose Michael Curtiz as director, cast Ingrid Bergman as Ilsa, and ensured that every cameo role featured the most suitable actor to play it. He also cast the role that would forever change Humphrey Bogart's screen persona, from hardened criminal to romantic lead. A number of the lines, including 'Of all the gin joints, in all the towns, in all the world, she walks into mine', and 'Here's looking at you, kid', were actually written by Bogart. And contrary to popular belief, none of the characters say, 'Play it again, Sam'.

CITIZEN KANE

Director: Orson Welles

Year: 1941

Starring: Orson Welles, Joseph Cotten, Dorothy Comingore, Erskine Sanford, Agnes Moorehead, Everett Sloane, Ruth Warrick

The critics' favourite, *Citizen Kane* has topped 'best of' polls more than any other film. It charts the story of Charles Foster Kane's life, after his death, through the eyes of those who knew, and both loved and hated him. At the heart of the story is the mystery over the word he spoke with his dying breath, 'Rosebud'. It is key to understanding the man and what drove him. Welles's film is radical in so many ways. Firstly, Hollywood gave the 26-year-old unprecedented control over a sizeable production, including final cut. Welles employed Greg Toland, who revolutionised cinematography with what became known as deep focus, which allowed both the foreground and background to appear sharp to the eye. And the film's script was not only daring, it was loosely based on the life of media magnate William Randolph Hearst, one of the pioneers of the 'yellow' press, the more scurrilous and muck-raking form of journalism, whose attempts to start a war between America and Spain are mirrored in the film. Hearst was furious that *Citizen Kane* had been made and attempted to buy all copies of the film print so he could destroy them. Thankfully for us, he failed.

61

ROSEBUD SLED

An early scene in *Citizen Kane* plays a key role in understanding Orson Welles's eponymous anti-hero. Young Kane plays on his sled in the snow before he is wrenched away from his family and sent to boarding school. However, its importance will be lost to the world because 'Rosebud', as the boy called it, is placed on a bonfire following his death. It represented happiness for him. The swindling media magnate is the dark side that emerges from this lost world of his youth.

AMÉLIE

Director: Jean-Pierre Jeunet

Year: 2001

Starring: Audrey Tautou, Matthieu Kassovitz, Rufus, Lorella Cravotta, Jamel Debbouze

Amélie is the story of an ordinary Parisian girl who stole the cinema-going world's heart and made the actress playing her a star. Jean-Pierre Jeunet's modern-day fairy-tale details what happens when his eponymous heroine discovers a box of personal treasures hidden in a wall. Retrieving it, she vows to spend her life making people happy if the box's owner is pleased with its return, which he is. She then reunites estranged lovers, repairs the sadness in people's lives and finally encourages her father to travel the world, with the help of a garden gnome and a friendly airhostess. However, Amélie herself is lonely. She potentially finds love, in the form of Matthieu Kassovitz's eccentric photographer, but does she have the courage to follow through on her own dreams of happiness? Audrey Tautou's charismatic performance takes the definition of kooky to a new level, yet always keeps us on her side. The script, which is occasionally so sweet a diabetic may think twice before indulging in it, certainly has fun playing with Parisian stereotypes. As for Jeunet, the director spirits us on a magical journey through the lesser-known areas of the French capital with a breathless energy. *Vive le cinéma*!

PULP FICTION

Director: Quentin Tarantino
Year: 1994
Starring: John Travolta, Samuel L. Jackson. Uma Thurman, Bruce Willis, Ving Rhames, Rosanna Arquette, Tim Roth, Amanda Plummer

There was nothing cooler in 1990s cinema than Quentin Tarantino. And of all his films, *Pulp Fiction* remains the coolest. It is a post-modern pulp crime drama, played out by A-list stars, with more than a dash of blood-splattering violence, and lines of dialogue that have since become an integral part of popular culture. Three stories are linked out of chronological order: two henchmen are ordered by their boss to kill some boys who have duped him out of a prize possession; one of the henchmen is ordered to look after the boss's wife for the night, only for her to overdose on heroin; and a boxer who refuses to throw a fight ends up in a compromising situation with the same gang boss. The film resuscitated the careers of Bruce Willis and John Travolta, who shows off his dance skills once again, this time with Uma Thurman. And it made a star out of Samuel L. Jackson, who steals the film from everyone by quoting the bible, sporting a mean set of sideburns and enjoying the sound of that most European of fast food dishes: the Royale with cheese.

ROCKY

Director: John G. Avildson

Year: 1976

Starring: Sylvester Stallone, Burgess Meredith, Talia Shire, Burt Young, Carl Weathers

The underdog winner of the Oscar for Best Picture in 1977, *Rocky* is a traditional rags to riches tale. Written by its star, it chronicles what happens when a once-promising boxer, now a well-meaning enforcer for a Philly loan shark, gets a shot at the big time when the manager of the world heavyweight champion, Apollo Creed, decides to stage a David and Goliath promotional fight. Although the film is best remembered by many for its punishing fight sequence, which would eventually dominate most of the sequels' running time, what is most striking about this first outing for the Italian Stallion is the attention it pays to blue-collar life. Alongside this is the now familiar training montage, with Rocky working out in different locations, from the gym owned by his manager Mickey, to a meat market where he pummels someone's Sunday roast. The montage reaches its climax, to the strains of the film's theme song, 'Gonna Fly Now', with Rocky running up the steps to the Philadelphia Museum of Modern Art. All that remains is the fight with Creed, which features more fake blood than the average war movie.

SPARTACUS

Director: Stanley Kubrick

Year: 1960

Starring: Kirk Douglas, Jean Simmons, Laurence Olivier, Tony Curtis, Peter Ustinov, Charles Laughton, John Gavin

Stanley Kubrick's foray into the Hollywood epic was a favour to its producer-star Kirk Douglas, who appeared in his 1957 anti-war drama *Paths of Glory* and needed a filmmaker with vision following his sacking of the previous director, Anthony Mann. It tells the story of an uprising by a group of gladiators in the first century BC, who become a symbol of freedom for slaves throughout Italy. Roman Senator Marcus Crassus uses the uprising to gain unprecedented powers, with which he eventually crushes the rebellion, but fails to dim the spirit of the rebels. When the captured survivors of the climactic battle are told they are free if their leader identifies himself, no sooner has Spartacus stood up than every man joins him to cry out 'I am Spartacus'. All are crucified and left to die, but not before Spartacus sees the woman he loves and their baby escape to freedom. With its exciting battles, a powerful script by the then blacklisted writer Dalton Trumbo, and superb performances by the cast, *Spartacus* is rightly regarded as one of Hollywood's best epics.

THE GOOD, THE BAD AND THE UGLY

Director: Sergio Leone

Year: 1966

Starring: Clint Eastwood, Eli Wallach, Lee Van Cleef

The man with no name returns in the final instalment of maverick Italian director Sergio Leone's Dollar Trilogy. In the dying days of the American Civil War, a Yankee wagon containing a chest of gold goes missing. Tuco, a good-for-nothing bandit, knows the cemetery it is buried in. Angel Eyes extracts the information from him and sets out to get it himself. But only Blondie, as Tuco refers to the quick-to-draw stranger, knows under which gravestone they can find it. So begins their journey across a war-ravaged landscape. In many ways the bridge between the smaller scale *A Fistful of Dollars* (1964) and *For a Few Dollars More* (1965), and the more expansive *Once Upon a Time in the West* (1968), Leone's final film with Clint Eastwood is a masterpiece in its own right. The star, who was best known for his role in the TV series *Rawhide* before Leone cast him in the first of his spaghetti westerns, delivers a coolly laconic performance that would become the template for the remainder of his career. Eli Wallach's Tuco brings complexity to what could have been a superficial character, and Lee Van Cleef was never better as the sadistic baddie.

CANNON

Humour is a key component of Sergio Leone's epic western, nowhere more so than in the relationship between Blondie and Tuco. When the bandit attempts to escape from Blondie, thinking he knows the name of the grave where the gold is buried, the cool gunfighter trains a cannon on him. The explosion sends Tuco flying into the air and landing against a gravestone on the edge of the cemetery the men have been searching for, leading us into the film's thrilling climax.

THE GODFATHER

Director: Francis Ford Coppola

Year: 1972

Starring: Marlon Brando, Al Pacino, James Caan, Diane Keaton, Robert Duvall, Talia Shire, Sterling Hayden

Francis Ford Coppola transformed Mario Puzo's pulpy best seller about a Mafia clan into a work of art. The story chronicles the passing of power from an older generation to a more ruthless new breed of gangster. When Michael Corleone succeeds his father Vito, we witness a shrewd and calculating man execute all opponents, no matter how close to him or his family they are, in order to pave the way for a new era. Coppola's genius was to elevate the drama to the scale of a grand opera. Marlon Brando made one of cinema's great comebacks as Vito, a role that Frank Sinatra desperately wanted. Al Pacino cemented his position as one of new Hollywood's finest young actors. And the relatively young Coppola showed he could command a sizeable production. Like the gangster films of the 1930s, The Godfather is supremely entertaining in the way it draws us into this deadly but exciting world. (The true cost of power is explored more in the film's 1974 sequel.) Just don't watch the film if you're a fan of horses!

TITANIC

Director: James Cameron

Year: 1997

Starring: Leonardo DiCaprio, Kate Winslet, Frances Fisher, Billy Zane, Kathy Baker, David Warner, Bernard Hill, Bill Paxton

It cost over £100 million to produce and featured two relatively well-known actors, but not the kind of stars that could command major box office returns. Moreover, we all know what happens in the end. So how did *Titanic* become the biggest box office success of all time? James Cameron's solution to how the film ends lies in focusing on the love story between Jack and Rose. She tells us the story in flashback, as an old woman, so audiences are left to wonder what happened to the young Irish lad who wins passage on the ship. Aboard, Jack falls in love with Rose, who is above his station and whose mother has planned a marriage for her that will benefit them financially. Younger audiences would be captivated by the romance, while everyone else paid – more than once – to see the seemingly indestructible symbol of the modern age sunk by an iceberg. And what a sight it is. From the iconic 'king of the world' moment on the ship's bow, to witnessing the huge vessel submerge beneath the waves, Cameron's film is a grand undertaking that would eventually win 11 Oscars, equaling *Ben-Hur*'s (1959) record.

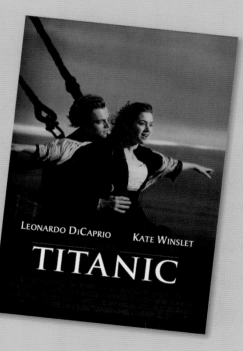

THE USUAL SUSPECTS

Director: Bryan Singer

Year: 1995

Starring: Gabriel Byrne, Kevin Spacey, Benicio Del Toro, Stephen Baldwin, Kevin Pollack, Chaz Palminteri, Suzy Amis, Pete Postlethwaite

Five men are forced to take part in a line-up for a crime they had no involvement in. However, the chance encounter prompts a partnership that begins with a heist in New York and ends with them coming as close as anyone ever has to the true face of evil, the criminal mastermind Keyser Söze. Told in flashback to an FBI agent by Verbal Kint, one of the five men, what unfolds is a tale of double-crossing and murder that might finally reveal the face of the devil himself. Director Bryan Singer and the strong cast bring Christopher McQuarrie's zigzagging script thrillingly to life. Benicio Del Toro was a relative unknown before the film was released, while Kevin Spacey's Oscar-winning turn as Verbal made him a star. However, the real draw of the film, which might explain its success, is the mysterious character of Söze. His story taps into our love of myth, even if such a character could never be real. Or perhaps he is. As Verbal tells us, 'The greatest trick the devil ever pulled was convincing the world he didn't exist.'

THE BOURNE IDENTITY

Director: Doug Liman

Year: 2002

Starring: Matt Damon, Franka Potenta, Chris Cooper, Brian Cox, Clive Owen, Julia Stiles

A body is found drifting out to sea by a group of fishermen. Barely alive and riddled with bullet holes, the man is saved by the ship's doctor, but when he awakens he has no memory of who he is or why he has been shot. So begins the story of Jason Bourne, an assassin for the American government, who is injured when an operation goes wrong. His next mission is to find out his identity, but in doing so he not only places himself in the firing line of his enemies, he becomes a target for the people he works for. Director Doug Liman was inspired to adapt Robert Ludlum's best seller by his father's career at the NSA. The story was adapted for a post-9/11 world and the fight scenes, pared down from the high explosive antics of action movies from the 1980s and 1990s, were more focused on hand-to-hand combat. The film's success made an action star out of Matt Damon, resulted in two equally popular sequels and even inspired the re-boot of the Bond franchise, with *Casino Royale* (2006) adopting a similar less-is-more approach.

CROUCHING TIGER,
HIDDEN DRAGON

Director: Ang Lee

Year: 2000

Starring: Chow Yun-fat, Michelle Yeoh, Ziyi Zhang, Chen Chang, Pei-pei Cheng

Magic, romance and kick-ass fight scenes combine in Ang Lee's breathtaking Oscar winner, set during the Qing Dynasty in the 18th century. New star Ziyi Zhang plays Jen, a young woman fed up with her role as the daughter of a regional lord, and who desires a more exciting life. When she steals the legendary Green Destiny Sword, its owner, Li Mu Bai, pursues her. As a result of the theft, the legendary warrior will finally face his old adversary Jade Fox in a battle to the death. Lee's film, with his flying characters (created through a combination of traditional wirework and CGI effects), tales of romance, court intrigue and banditry, is a magical journey across the Chinese landscape, culminating in a stunning battle between Jen and Li Mu Bai atop a densely wooded forest.

DIE HARD

Director: John McTiernan

Year: 1988

Starring: Bruce Willis, Alan Brickman, Bonnie Bedelia, Alexander Godunov, Reginald VelJohnson

The best of the 1980s blockbusters, which made Bruce Willis an international star, *Die Hard* also proved that mainstream action movies could show a little intelligence. Willis plays John McClane, a New York cop visiting his estranged wife in Los Angeles for the holidays, who is invited to her company's Christmas party in a newly built skyscraper. However, a gang of well-armed, well-dressed and mostly European thieves soon overruns it. They are intent on stealing a fortune in bearer bonds and their only obstacle is McClane, who soon gains the upper hand. With its sly humour, terrific pace and effectively staged set pieces, *Die Hard* set a high standard for the action movie. Over the course of another four films (one good, two average, and a truly awful fifth instalment), McClane is to Bruce Willis what Dirty Harry is to Clint Eastwood. It is hard to believe that Arnold Schwarzenegger was originally considered for the role, let alone Frank Sinatra! But the film's secret weapon is Alan Brickman, as the suave, smooth-talking and ruthlessly efficient villain, Hans Gruber. He steals every scene, including the film's climax and his fall from disgrace.

DR. NO

Director: Terrence Young

Year: 1962

Starring: Sean Connery, Ursula Andress, Bernard Lee, Joseph Wiseman, Jack Lord

The first adaptation of Ian Fleming's popular spy series set the template for the films that would follow: stunning locations, glamorous women and a dashing hero as versed in delivering one-liners as he is skilled in defeating his adversaries, who, like Dr. No, have to be stopped from holding the world to ransom. No matter that a Scotsman was cast in a quintessentially English role. (It initially mattered for Fleming, who only saw in Sean Connery 'an overgrown stuntman'. He later changed his mind and incorporated a Scottish back-story for Bond.) *Dr. No* reinvented the action film and gave audiences a less morally upstanding figure to the ones they had been used to. This was the beginning of the Swinging Sixties and attitudes were changing, which allowed the producers to cast a scantily clad Ursula Andress as Honey Rider. Her memorable entrance in the film, coming out of the sea in a white bikini, is one of the defining images of the decade.

KING KONG

Director: Marian C. Cooper

Year: 1933

Starring: Fay Wray, Robert Armstrong, Bruce Cabot, Frank Reicher, Sam Hardy

Fay Wray became an overnight star playing Ann Darrow, an unemployed actress who joins a film crew shooting an action adventure film on a mysterious uncharted island. No sooner has she stepped on it when Ann is kidnapped by natives and sacrificed to the mighty Kong, an immense ape who, for some reason, is fascinated by her. She is eventually rescued by her colleagues, and Kong is captured and taken to New York, where he becomes a huge attraction. However, he breaks free of his shackles, finds Ann and seeks refuge at the top of the Empire State Building, from which he eventually falls to his death. A variation on the beauty and the beast story, with remarkable special effects for its time, this version of the film remains superior to the subsequent remakes. The immense gates that were built for Kong's enclosure made one final appearance on film, as a collapsing building during the burning of Atlanta in *Gone with the Wind* (1939). And if you're ever going to see some strange beast at the circus, do not believe anyone who calls out to the audience, 'Don't be alarmed, ladies and gentlemen. Those chains are made of chrome steel.'

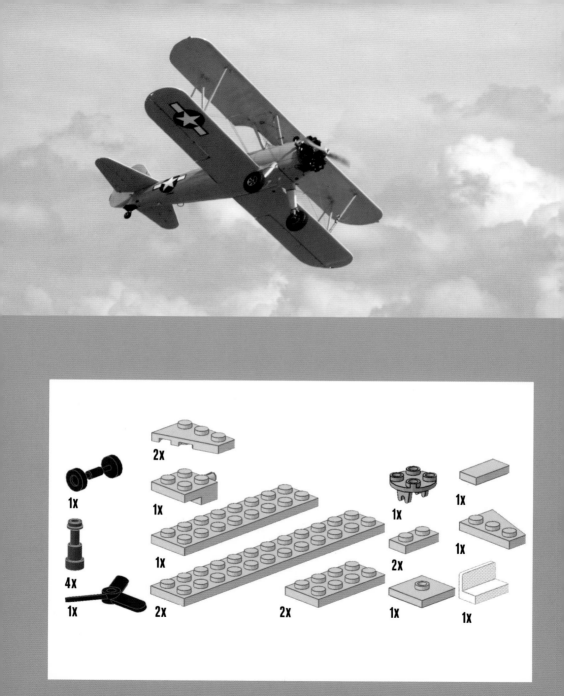

BIPLANE

The climactic moments of *King Kong* remain one of the most famous scenes in cinema history. It was created using a combination of actual footage, model sets and stop-motion technology, whereby the model of Kong had its position changed every frame so that when the film plays it looks like the creature is moving. But what makes this sequence so memorable is that we are on the side of the beast, and its fall is not so much a triumph for the biplane pilots who shoot it down as a sense of sadness that the creature is no more.

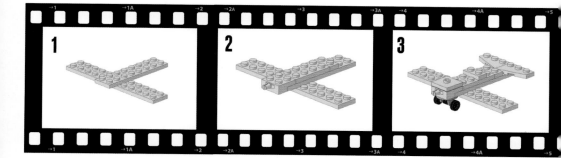

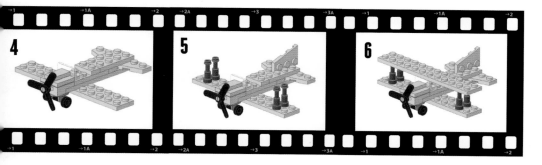

GLADIATOR

Director: Ridley Scott

Year: 2000

Starring: Russell Crowe, Joaquin Phoenix, Richard Harris, Connie Nielsen, Oliver Reed

Russell Crowe is Maximus, father to a murdered son, husband to a murdered wife, and he will have his revenge on Joaquin Phoenix's selfish tyrant Commodus. Crowe has said that of all the roles he has played, the betrayed general of the Roman army who becomes a gladiator in order to win back his honour, his country and to avenge his family, is his favourite. He's convincing in the role, particularly in the gladiatorial ring, both in Africa and then in the Italian capital's mighty Coliseum, which was re-created on a much larger scale using digital technology. Historical fact takes a back seat for the story. Commodus was actually regarded as a benevolent leader and loved by his army. However, changing history has never got in the way of a ripping Hollywood blockbuster and, accuracy aside, Ridley Scott's film is one of the most enjoyable and thrilling epics of recent times.

INDEPENDENCE DAY

Director: Roland Emmerich

Year: 1996

Starring: Will Smith, Jeff Goldblum, Bill Pullman, Mary McDonnell, Judd Hirsch, Margaret Colin

Has the end of the world as we know it ever been as entertaining as Roland Emmerich's sci-fi disaster movie? When a vast number of alien spacecraft descend into the earth's atmosphere, only Jeff Goldblum's computer whiz David Levinson realises that the strange transmission blocking the world's communications is a countdown. With the president alerted, people are ordered to evacuate the cities, but it is too late for most. After the stunning attack sequence, which sees a host of American landmarks being obliterated, *Independence Day* focuses on humanity's fight back. Well, America's actually, as it looks like the world is waiting on Bill Pullman's president to make the first move, which he does with the help of David's plan and Will Smith's crack pilot. The film saw Smith's star soar into the stratosphere thanks in no small part to his on-screen charisma, while the film now ranks as a sci-fi classic.

JURASSIC PARK

Director: Steven Spielberg

Year: 1993

Starring: Sam Neill, Laura Dern, Jeff Goldblum, Richard Attenborough, Bob Peck, Samuel L. Jackson

Two palaeontologists and a chaotician arrive on an island near Costa Rica, belonging to bioengineering magnate Dr John Hammond. Lured by the promise of a once-in-a-lifetime experience, what they discover is a landscape populated by dinosaurs that have been extinct for millennia. Hammond has successfully cloned thousands of species, which include a Tyrannosaurus Rex and deadly Velociraptors, intending to feature them as part of a theme park. However, as night falls, a violent storm approaches and, through the greed of one employee, the security fences fail, leaving all on the island easy prey for the voracious carnivores. Steven Spielberg's adaptation of Michael Crichton's best selling novel balances blockbuster thrills with discussions concerning the impact of scientific advances upon society, both ethically and morally. It also features groundbreaking special effects. The passage of time and advancement of digital technology may have lessened the initial impact of seeing a huge herbivore rising on its hind legs to eat leaves from the top of a tree. But the sight of a Tyrannosaurus Rex charging after a jeep down a muddy track still sets the heart racing.

99

ACTION AND ADVENTURE

RAIDERS OF THE LOST ARK

Director: Steven Spielberg

Year: 1981

Starring: Harrison Ford, Karen Allen, Paul Freeman, Denholm Elliott, John Rhys-Davies

Inspired by the serials that used to play before main features in cinemas in the 1930s and 1940s, Steven Spielberg's ripping yarn pits Harrison Ford's archaeologist adventurer Indiana Jones against the Nazis in a fast-paced race to uncover the location of the Ark of the Covenant. The idea for the film was originally conceived by George Lucas, who convinced Spielberg to direct it while they were taking a break in Hawaii after completing, respectively, *Star Wars* and *Close Encounters of the Third Kind* (1977). It was Spielberg who changed the main character's surname from Smith to Jones, while Indiana was the name of Lucas's Alaskan Malamute, whose features also inspired the creation of Chewbacca. Even though many studios turned down the project, stating that it would cost too much and there was no audience for it, Spielberg eventually brought the film in under budget and millions turned out to see it, making it the top-grossing film of the year. It now ranks as one of the director's best-loved films, thanks in no small part to the superb opening sequence that sees Indy recover an ancient golden relic, only to be chased by a massive boulder and spear-wielding natives.

THE
TERMINATOR

Director: James Cameron

Year: 1984

Starring: Arnold Schwarzenegger, Linda Hamilton, Michael Biehn, Lance Henriksen

A man and a robot are sent from the future to present-day Los Angeles. The robot, a seemingly indestructible cyborg, has orders to kill Sarah Conner, the mother of the man who will lead the resistance against a computer network that takes over the world and nearly obliterates humankind. The other time-traveller is Kyle Reese, sent to protect Sarah. So begins a terrific sci-fi movie and the rise of Arnold Schwarzenegger as one of the biggest – literally – movie stars ever to pack an Uzi 9mm, and with biceps the width of a small cow. It also cemented James Cameron's position as one of Hollywood's more talented filmmakers, who recognised the problems of his star's thick Austrian accent and turned it to his favour with a script that featured minimal dialogue. Nevertheless, there are still a number of memorable lines, including 'I'll be back', a promise Arnie kept when he returned, albeit as a hero, for Cameron's stunning 1991 sequel.

LIFE OF PI

Director: Ang Lee

Year: 2012

Starring: Suraj Sharma, Irrfan Khan, Rafe Spall, Gérard Depardieu, Tabu

Ang Lee's visually dazzling film is based on Yann Martel's award-winning novel. A young Indian boy finds himself in a lifeboat following the sinking of the ship that was transporting his family and the zoo they once owned from India to Canada. The only other survivors are an orangutan and injured zebra, but a voracious hyena soon eats those. However, that's only when Pi's problems really begin, for the hyena is then consumed by Richard Parker, the name the boy gives to the Bengal tiger that has been hiding under the boat's tarpaulin. Lee's film, which makes innovative use of 3D and visual effects to create a world that is, in turn, magical and threatening, successfully balances the source novel's theological themes with one of the most original of Robinson Crusoe tales. The world's largest self-generating wave tank, built at a disused Taiwanese airport and holding almost two million gallons of water, was where most of the film was shot. But the greatest achievement is the creation of Richard Parker. Brought to life by state-of-the-art computer effects, he is a magnificent sight.

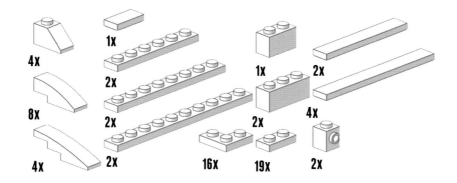

PI'S BOAT

The name Richard Parker is taken from the Edgar Allan Poe novel, *The Narrative of Arthur Gordon Pym on Nantucket*. He is a mutineer on a vessel that becomes shipwrecked, who advocates cannibalism in order to survive. (Interestingly, Pym's dog is called Tiger.) It is a fitting name for the creature that both hounds Pi on his lonely journey across the Indian Ocean and is the reason for his survival. How they co-exist becomes clear in the story's final stages, which blur the line between truth and allegory, underpinning Yann Martel's exploration of faith and religious belief.

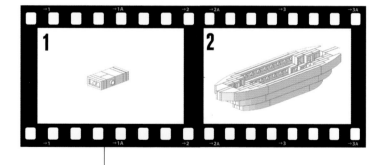

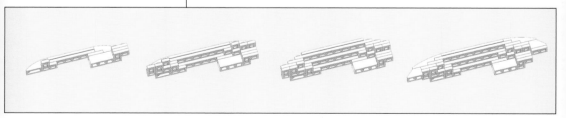

THE MATRIX

Directors: Andy Wachowski, Lana Wachowski

Year: 1999

Starring: Keanu Reeves, Carrie-Anne Moss, Laurence Fishburne, Hugo Weaving, Joe Pantoliano

What if the world we live in is actually a dream created by computers in order to control us, and what would we do if we woke up one day and actually realised this? Welcome to the world of Thomas Anderson, aka. Neo. By day he is a computer programmer for a big corporation, but at night he attempts to hack his way into a system called the Matrix. When he meets the mysterious Trinity and Morpheus, his eyes are opened to the 'desert of the real', in which a computer system has taken over the world. With the aid of his new friends, Neo sets out to destroy it, thanks in no small part to his being programmed with every kind of martial art, equipped with an arsenal of weapons that your local survivalist would be jealous of and a wardrobe of black and leather that makes him the coolest-looking action hero. The actors trained solidly for four months to reach an acceptable level of martial artistry for the fight scenes, while the Oscar-winning Bullet Time effect, which sees characters suspended in mid-air, has influenced countless other films.

BACK TO THE FUTURE

Director: Robert Zemeckis

Year: 1985

Starring: Michael J. Fox, Christopher Lloyd, Lea Thompson, Crispin Glover

Nothing seems to be working out for Marty McFly. He doesn't connect with his family, his neighbour bullies his father and life holds no excitement. Then his friend Doc, a mad scientist and inventor, unveils a car that can travel in time, just before he is killed by terrorists. Marty ends up travelling back to 1955, where he must ensure that his parents get together, while finding a way back to the future and saving his friend. The perfect vehicle for launching the immensely likeable Michael J. Fox's film career, *Back to the Future* will forever be associated with the 1980s thanks to the appearance of one of the decade's most iconic symbols of excess: the DeLorean car. Zemeckis's adventure comedy also makes the most of the cultural differences between the two periods. And, like his later *Forrest Gump* (1994), the film adopts a playful approach to American history, a factor that becomes more evident, and complex, in the sequels that followed.

FLUX CAPACITOR

The flux capacitor is the legendary scientific breakthrough that allows time travel to be possible. In the movie it is shown affixed to the DeLorean between the two front seats. Doc comes up with the flux capacitor after falling and knocking himself out on his bathroom sink and he spends the next few decades working out how to power it. *Back to the Future* joins Marty and Doc on their quest to obtain plutonium to cause a nuclear reaction big enough to produce '1.21 jigawatts' of electrical power to charge the device and push them through the space–time continuum.

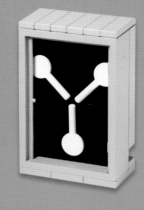

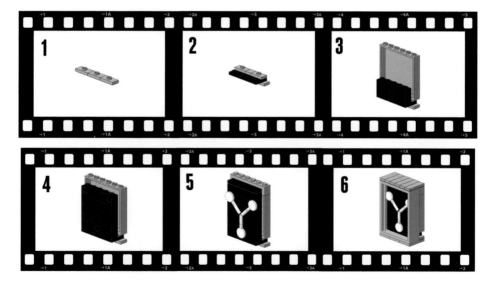

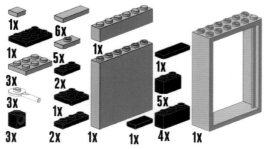

THE ITALIAN JOB

Director: Peter Collinson

Year: 1969

Starring: Michael Caine, Noël Coward, Benny Hill, Rossano Brazzi

London at the height of the Swinging Sixties is the backdrop to this much-loved caper movie. Noël Coward is an unlikely gangland boss who commissions Michael Caine's heist expert Charlie Crocker to carry out a daring robbery in the Italian city of Turin during a soccer match between England and Italy. His team is comprised of getaway drivers (Caine himself couldn't actually drive when the film was shot), thieves and Benny Hill's computer expert, whose obsession with large women will risk the entire operation. With memorable lines like 'You're only supposed to blow the bloody doors off', and Quincy Jones's closing song 'Get a Bloomin' Move On' (aka 'The Self Preservation Society'), performed by the cast, the film has become an icon of the era. And some credit should perhaps go to the Mafia. They were responsible for closing many of Turin's roadways when the city's authorities refused to give the production a filming permit.

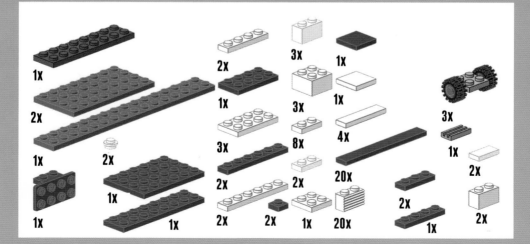

HARRINGTON LEGIONNAIRE BUS

When filming began, *The Italian Job* didn't have an ending. And not everyone making the film liked the one the writers came up with. The closing moments literally end on a cliffhanger, with Charlie Crocker crawling along the floor of the thieves' bus in an attempt to save the stolen gold from falling out of the back door and down the mountain. As all seems lost, Charlie utters the classic line, 'Hang on, lads; I've got a great idea'. The camera pulls away, leaving them there and the audience in a state of suspense.

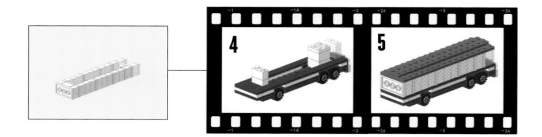

LARA CROFT: TOMB RAIDER

Director: Simon West

Year: 2001

Starring: Angelina Jolie, John Voight, Daniel Craig, Iain Glenn, Noah Taylor

The journey from computer game to big screen is a perilous one, with few film adaptations ever making the grade. Some may have been disappointed with the end results of *Lara Croft: Tomb Raider*, but few were unhappy with the choice of actress to play the eponymous action heroine. With her bee-stung lips and athletic physique, Angelina Jolie is the living embodiment of Lara. The story revolves around the desperate race to find the Triangle of Light, a mystical object that will give immeasurable power to whomever possesses it. Lara knows it relates to the disappearance of her father and sets out to find it, but is pursued by representatives from the secretive Illuminati, who desire the artefact for their own ends. A poor man's Indiana Jones, the film is saved by Jolie, whose charisma shines in every scene and whose playful performance suggests that she is fully aware of the nonsensical premise of the story, but is nonetheless having a ball kicking everyone's ass.

NIGHT AT THE MUSEUM

Director: Shawn Levy

Year: 2006

Starring: Ben Stiller, Robin Williams, Mizuo Peck, Steve Coogan, Ricky Gervais, Dick Van Dyke, Mickey Rooney, Bill Cobbs

An old-fashioned yarn is given a makeover thanks to some fantastic visual effects. Desperate for his son's respect, failed entrepreneur Larry Davy takes a job as a night watchman at the American Museum of Natural History. On his first shift he discovers that all the artefacts – human, animal and, in the case of a Tyrannosaurus Rex, skeletal – come to life. He finds out from Teddy Roosevelt that this has happened every night since 1952, when an ancient Egyptian relic arrived at the museum. However, unbeknown to Larry, there are plans afoot to steal it. Shawn Levy's film, aimed squarely at a family audience, is a madcap adventure reminiscent of older Disney films such as *One of Our Dinosaurs is Missing* (1975), albeit with fewer nuances. There are numerous cameos, including Robin Williams' ex-president, Ricky Gervais's annoying administrator, and Steve Coogan and Owen Wilson playing squabbling, pint-sized models of a Roman centurion and cowboy, who join forces with Larry to prevent the theft.

AUSTIN POWERS: INTERNATIONAL MAN OF MYSTERY

Director: Jay Roach

Year: 1997

Starring: Mike Myers, Elizabeth Hurley, Michael York, Mimi Rogers, Robert Wagner, Seth Green

Parody is too conservative a word to describe Mike Myers' spoof of the 1960s spy genre. Austin Powers, a relic of the Cold War, who was cryogenically frozen at the end of it, is thawed out when his arch nemesis Dr Evil returns to threaten mankind. With the aid of Vanessa Kensington, the daughter of his old sidekick, and the stiff-upper-lipped Basil Exposition, Austin sets out to defeat his old foe. Myers plays both the hero and villain in the film, which opens with arguably the best comedy song and dance number since the 'Every Sperm is Sacred' sequence in Monty Python's *The Meaning of Life* (1983). There are not-so-subtle references to the inanely sexist female character names from the Bond films (most outrageously, Alotta Fagina), and too many great catchphrases to list here. Quite simply groovy, baby.

THE BLUES BROTHERS

Director: John Landis

Year: 1980

Starring: John Belushi, Dan Aykroyd, Carrie Fisher, Cab Calloway, James Brown, Ray Charles, Aretha Franklin

Take two anarchic comedians, feature a line-up of legendary R'n'B stars, include the most insane car chase in Hollywood history and you have the basic ingredients of John Landis's madcap tale of two blues-lovin' brothers. Developed from characters created for *Saturday Night Live* by John Belushi and Dan Aykroyd, the film opens with Elwood picking up his brother Jake from prison. Before long, they are being pursued by half the state's law enforcement agencies, a bitter and well-armed ex-girlfriend, a country and western band from whom the brothers stole a gig, and angry members of the Illinois Nazi Party, all the while being on a 'mission from God' to save the orphanage they were raised in from closure. When the possibility of a *Blues Brothers* film first surfaced, there was a bidding war in Hollywood, even though no script had been written. The film would eventually rocket past its original budget and fall seriously behind schedule. No matter. The film was a modest success when it was released, but has since achieved a huge following. The leads' deadpan performances contrast brilliantly with the chaos around them, while James Brown, Aretha Franklin, Ray Charles and Cab Calloway shine in their respective performances.

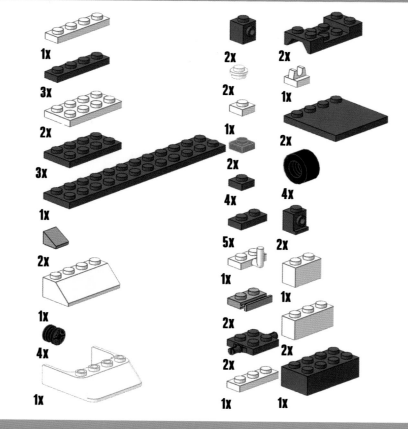

POLICE CAR

A key character in *The Blues Brothers* is the Bluesmobile, Elwood's battered and dishevelled Dodge Monaco police car from the Mount Prospect district of Illinois. In actuality, 13 cars, all bought from an auction held by the California Highway Patrol, stood in for the vehicle that helps the brothers evade an army of cars, vans and trucks. At the time of its release, *The Blues Brothers* won the world record for the most cars destroyed in one film. It was surpassed by its 1998 sequel.

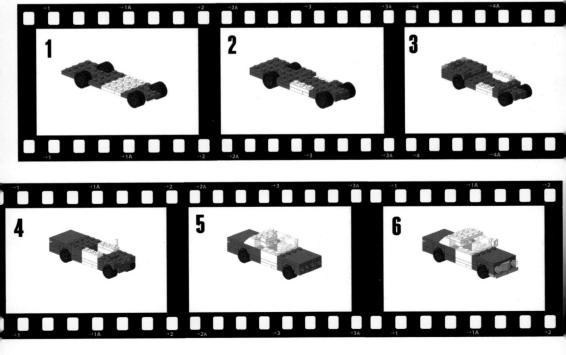

127

DIRTY DANCING

Director: Emile Ardolino

Year: 1987

Starring: Patrick Swayze, Jennifer Grey, Jerry Orbach, Cynthia Rhodes, Jack Weston

It's the summer of 1963 and Frances 'Baby' Houseman travels with her family to Kellerman's, a rural summer resort. Initially bored, she changes her opinion of the place when she sees two dance teachers and their friends cavorting at an after-hours staff party. Frances soon becomes part of the group and, when Johnny's dance partner is unable to partake in the season's closing review with him, she jumps in. Her father is unimpressed, but as Johnny tells him, 'Nobody puts Baby in the corner'. Screenwriter Eleanor Bergstein had written just one screenplay before *Dirty Dancing* and based most of the story on her own childhood experiences. Filmmaker Emile Ardolino had won an Oscar for the 1983 documentary *He Makes Me Feel Like Dancin'*, but had never made a feature. Patrick Swayze had trained with the Joffrey Ballet Company, but was better known in cinema for action roles. And though Jennifer Grey had also trained as a dancer, she was most famous for playing Ferris Bueller's sister. And yet, all these components, combined with a best-selling soundtrack that included the Oscar-winning song 'The Time of My Life', made for box office gold around the world.

FERRIS
BUELLER'S
DAY OFF

Director: John Hughes

Year: 1986

Starring: Matthew Broderick, Alan Ruck, Mia Sara, Jennifer Grey, Jeffrey Jones

John Hughes' tale of a teenager far more resourceful than the adults around him captures the excitement of youthful rebellion and is seen as one of the key movies of the 1980s. Ferris convinces his parents he is ill, while his schoolmates believe he is at death's door. He picks up his girlfriend Sloane, his best friend Cameron, and drives them, in Cameron's father's sports car, into Chicago for the day. However, Ferris's sister and the school principal are less convinced of his incapacitation. Written in just 10 days, Hughes' script favours character over plot. In Ferris, the writer-director created the teen rebel every kid wanted to be.

131

THE MUSIC BOX

Director: James Parrott

Year: 1932

Starring: Stan Laurel, Oliver Hardy

Down on their luck, Stan and Ollie empty their paltry bank account to set themselves up as deliverymen. Their first commission is delivering a piano to a house at the top of a long and steep series of steps. However, each attempt to ascend the staircase finds their way blocked, first by a nanny pushing a pram, then by a large man who, unbeknown to Stan and Ollie, is the unwitting recipient of the package. Each time, the piano ends up falling back to the bottom of the steps, and the pair's exasperation with the people they encounter gets them into trouble with the police. The simple set-up for this hilarious sketch was originated in the comedy duo's 1927 silent short *Hats Off*, which no longer exists. Of all their early films it is one of the most famous and best loved. The actual steps used still exist in Los Angeles, in Silver Lake District, near Laurel and Hardy Park, and are highlighted by a sign telling visitors of their importance in cinema history.

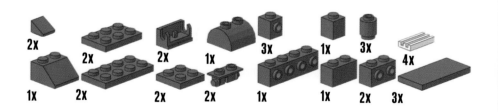

2x   2x   2x   1x   3x   1x   3x   4x

1x   2x   2x   2x   1x   1x   2x   3x

GRAND PIANO

The genius of Laurel and Hardy's Oscar-winning short lies in the choice of item being delivered. A piano is both heavy and delicate. Moreover, its musicality allowed the duo and director James Parrott to play around with the sound every time it slid out of their grasp and went careering down the steps. The box is empty in the shots of the duo carrying it up the steps, but a real piano was added for its descent, in order for the exact noises it made to be recorded.

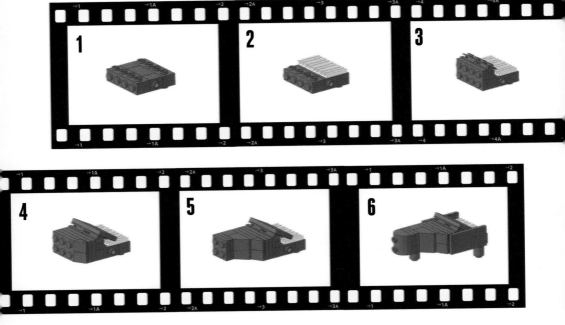

SINGIN' IN THE RAIN

Directors: Stanley Donen, Gene Kelly

Year: 1952

Starring: Gene Kelly, Debbie Reynolds, Cyd Charisse, Donald O'Connor, Jean Hagen

Singin' in the Rain is quite possibly the greatest musical ever produced and is certainly one of the best films about Hollywood. It focuses on that tumultuous period when sound was introduced into the movies. Don Lockwood and Lina Lamont are Hollywood's biggest stars, but the arrival of sound is causing problems for the studio. Not only is the technology disrupting filming, the actress has a voice no one will want to hear. Enter Debbie Reynolds' young ingénue, who might just be the perfect voice double. The only problem is that Don is falling in love with her. *Singin' in the Rain* seamlessly blends classic music numbers such as 'Make 'em Laugh', 'Moses Supposes' and the unforgettable title track, with stunning wordplay, physical comedy and a healthy dose of cynicism about the entertainment business. In particular, the scenes re-creating initial attempts to film with sound are hilarious, but also highlight the travails facing studios in adapting to the revolutionary new technology. And if there was ever an example of someone living up to the mantra of 'the show must go on', it is Kelly. He had a 39°C (103°F) fever when he performed 'Singin' in the Rain'.

SATURDAY NIGHT FEVER

Director: John Badham

Year: 1977

Starring: John Travolta, Karen Lynn Gorney, Barry Miller, Joseph Cali, Donna Pescow

Tony Manero (Travolta), a 19-year-old Brooklynite, lives with his parents and has a dead-end job at a hardware store. His one passion, which makes life worth living, lies in his skills as a disco dancer, which he shows off every Saturday night at the local nightclub, 2001 Odyssey. His usual partner is Annette (Donna Pescow), but when Stephanie (Karen Lynn Gorney) appears on the scene, Tony finally recognises someone who will help him win the top dancer prize. Like *Rocky* (1976), *Saturday Night Fever* is as much about the lives of a local community as it is the competition the main character wants to win. Local gangs, the camaraderie between young men, and the desperation to escape to a better life are central to the journey Tony undertakes. This less than pretty picture (the original version of the film was R-rated due to the bad language and scenes of sexual violence) stands in stark contrast to the music. Featuring key tracks by the Bee Gees, *Saturday Night Fever* became the defining film of the disco era, Tony's white suit was its key image and dancing would never ever be the same again.

MARY POPPINS

Director: Robert Stevenson

Year: 1964

Starring: Julie Andrews, Dick Van Dyke, David Tomlinson, Glynis Johns, Karen Dotrice, Matthew Garber, Elsa Lanchester

Julie Andrews became a star and won an Oscar playing the unconventional Edwardian nanny to Jane and Michael Banks. If only their parents knew she had flown down from the sky with the aid of her umbrella to take up the position. Unlike with previous nannies, the children take to her immediately, but their father is less convinced, questioning her influence over them. However, it is the parents' distance from their children that Mary Poppins has come to mend. Walt Disney's wish to adapt P. J. Traver's novel was recently the subject of the film *Saving Mr. Banks* (2013), and for all the author's reservations regarding the changes to her original story, Robert Stevenson's film retains a magical air. London here is as much a figment of the imagination as Poppins herself, the odd political reference to the times notwithstanding, such as Mrs Banks' involvement in the Suffragette movement and the rising influence of the banking industry over society. Ultimately, the song and dance numbers, as well as the sheer exuberance of the performances, are so good it is almost possible to forgive the film anything, even Dick Van Dyke's dreadful Cockney accent. Well, almost anything.

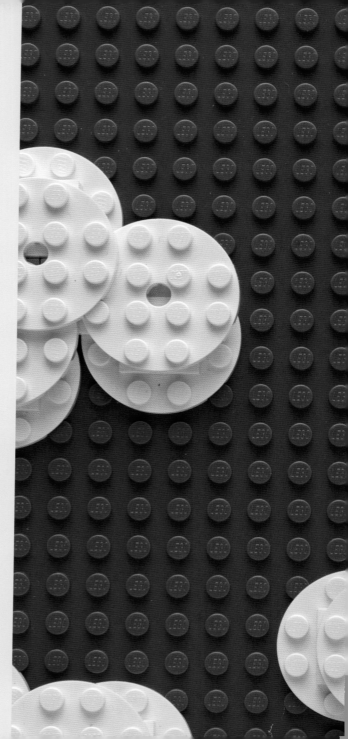

A NIGHT AT THE OPERA

Director: Sam Wood

Year: 1935

Starring: Groucho Marx, Chico Marx, Harpo Marx, Kitty Carlisle, Allan Jones

Not to be mistaken with the 1975 rock album by Queen, this was the first film to see the Marx Brothers' outfit reduced to three, following Zeppo's departure. The result, however, is no less zany than their earlier films. Groucho and Chico play two agents competing on behalf of a pair of opera singers, to secure them a key role in an upcoming production of Verdi's *Il Trovatore*. However, due to a series of mishaps, both find themselves duped and decide to take revenge. *A Night at the Opera* was the brothers' first film for MGM after leaving Paramount, and the studio head, Irving Thalberg, advised that their act could remain as madcap as ever, but their films required more story. The result is one of their most cohesive comedies, while still retaining an air of utter madness. Nowhere is this more evident than in the classic stateroom scene aboard a ship, which begins with Groucho ordering pretty much everything – including more than a dozen boiled eggs – off the breakfast menu, and ends with 15 people crammed tightly into a small cabin. It is cinema at its most absurd and inspired.

GREASE

Director: Randal Kleiser

Year: 1978

Starring: John Travolta, Olivia Newton John, Stockard Channing, Jeff Conway, Didi Conn, Eve Arden

Like *American Graffiti* (1973) before it, Randal Kleiser's exuberant musical looks back, through rose-tinted spectacles, to an earlier, more 'innocent' era. Newcomer Sandy arrives at Rydell High School, turning the heads of all the boys and sparking jealousy among the girls. In particular, she attracts the attention of Danny Zuko, the local bad boy and the last person this seeming goody two-shoes would ever be attracted to. However, we find out that during the previous summer they had a romance and the person Danny was then is not the badass he makes himself out to be to his gang. Thanks to the best-selling soundtrack that saw a number of singles top the charts, as well as its popularity among school and amateur theatre companies, *Grease* is not so much a film as a phenomenon. It made stars out of its leads, taught us that being square could be cool, and somehow managed to tame the teen movie, which had been raging against authority ever since James Dean appeared in *Rebel Without a Cause* (1955).

DOCTOR DOOLITTLE

Director: Richard Fleischer

Year: 1967

Starring: Rex Harrison, Samantha Eggar, Anthony Newley, Richard Attenborough, Peter Bull

An adaptation of Hugh Lofting's popular stories, *Doctor Doolittle* was Hollywood's attempt to cash in on the popularity of Rex Harrison after *My Fair Lady* (1964), and to make the most of a growing special effects industry. Doctor Doolittle escapes an asylum and sets off on an adventure that will see him travel the world, encounter and communicate with a host of animals.

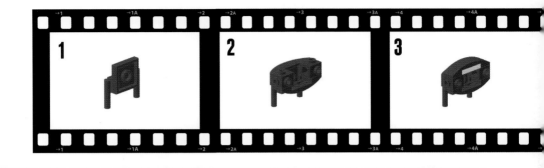

PUSHMI-PULLYU

Hugh Lofting's original vision of the pushmi-pullyu (pronounced 'push-me–pull-you') was a creature related to the gazelle, whose ancestor was the unicorn. It had two heads so that it could eat with one and talk with the other, thus never being impolite. In the film, it is closer to a llama, hence its origins in Tibet. It is able to communicate with the doctor because its dialect is close to that of the camel's, a language the learned medic has already mastered.

2x
2x
2x
2x
4x
4x
1x
4x

THE WIZARD OF OZ

Director: Victor Fleming

Year: 1939

Starring: Judy Garland, Frank Morgan, Ray Bolger, Bert Lahr, Jack Haley, Billie Burke, Margaret Hamilton

In the 1930s, fantasy films were a huge risk for studios, with no guarantee of a hit. So an adaptation of Frank L. Baum's tale of Dorothy, a young girl from Kansas, who travels to the wonderful world of Oz, meeting a host of strange and loveable characters, was not immediately considered to be audience friendly. What changed producers' minds was the runaway success of Disney's *Snow White and the Seven Dwarfs* (1937). However, the road to the film's completion was much longer than the one to Oz. Over ten writers were involved in creating the script and four filmmakers had a hand in directing it. Shirley Temple was the producer's original choice for Dorothy, and the casting for Lion, Tin Man and Scarecrow saw various changes. The special colour effects, still in their infancy, were a challenge, resulting in the film taking two years to complete. Most surprising of all is that one of the most famous moments of the film, Dorothy singing 'Over the Rainbow', almost didn't make the final cut.

THE SOUND OF MUSIC

Director: Robert Wise

Year: 1965

Starring: Julie Andrews, Christopher Plummer, Eleanor Parker, Richard Haydn

Few films are more beloved than this Rogers and Hammerstein musical. Carefree novice Maria is informed by her Mother Superior that she should take a sabbatical from convent life and is sent to the home of widower Captain Von Trapp, where she becomes governess to his seven children. They grow to love Maria, as does their father. However, with the rise of the Nazi party, Maria and the family find their lives under threat. The pleasure of Wise's film lies in its total immersion in this pre-war world. We are drawn in with a series of unforgettable songs, from the playful 'Do-Re-Me' and 'My Favourite Things', to 'Climb Every Mountain' and the bittersweet 'Edelweiss'. Christopher Plummer makes for a dashing captain and the young cast convince as a happy, though occasionally bickering, family. But the film belongs to Julie Andrews, whose joyous presence dominates. Cheesy? You only need to see the opening sequence and Andrews singing the title track from an Alpine meadow to answer that. Its campiness is why sing-along screenings of the film have become so popular. Not even the most die-hard cynic can resist it.

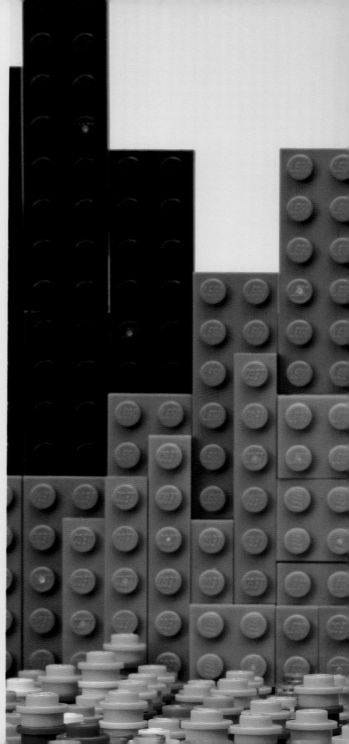

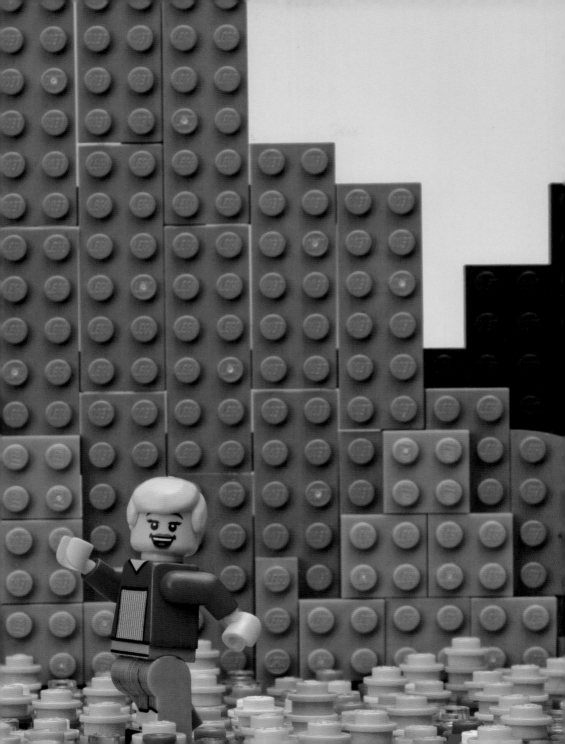

WEST SIDE STORY

Directors: Jerome Robbins, Robert Wise

Year: 1960

Starring: Natalie Wood, Richard Beymer, Russ Tamblyn, Rita Moreno, George Chakiris

Until *West Side Story*, the Hollywood musical was a clean-cut affair, with bright colours and exuberant numbers, accompanied by the odd ballad of longing. But then it all changed. First, with an aerial shot of a modern, overcrowded New York landscape, and then a story of gang warfare. Ostensibly an update of Shakespeare's *Romeo and Juliet*, Leonard Bernstein and Stephen Sondheim's musical is set in 1957 and pits a white American gang, the Jets, against a rival gang of Puerto Rican immigrants, the Sharks. The love affair between American Tony and Puerto Rican Maria, the younger sister of the Sharks' leader, Bernardo, exacerbates the gangs' territorial battles. Where the film excels is in how choreographer Jerome Robbins transforms the fight scenes into dance sequences. Even a simple walk across a street allows the characters to mark their territory through a series of graceful, yet threatening dance moves. It was a radical new form of musical, which would prove to be hugely influential. How different it might have been, however, had Elvis Presley accepted the role of Tony. His manager, Colonel Tom Parker, said no, a decision the singer would regret when the film won 10 Oscars.

FIRE ESCAPE

West Side Story's most obvious reference to *Romeo and Juliet* is also one of its highlights. Recalling the 'wherefore art thou' balcony scene from Act 2, Scene 2 of Shakespeare's play, Tony and Maria meet on a classic New York fire escape, outside her apartment block. There, in a passionate embrace, they sing one of the film's standout songs, 'Tonight', which seals their love and their fate. Although the film won 10 Oscars, neither Richard Beymer nor Natalie Wood was nominated. However, Wood did receive a nomination for her role in *Splendor in the Grass*, but lost to Sophia Loren.

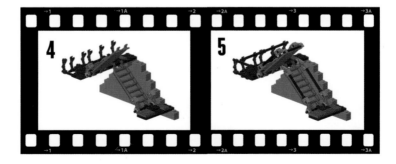

WAYNE'S WORLD

Director: Penelope Spheeris

Year: 1992

Starring: Mike Myers, Dana Carvey, Rob Lowe, Tia Carrere

The film that introduced the catchphrases 'Ex-squeeze me?', 'babelicious', 'schwing' and '…Not' into everyday language, *Wayne's World* is based on characters Mike Myers and Dana Carvey created for *Saturday Night Live*. The film's utterly nonsensical plot only highlights the fun to be had watching the comedians make the most of their twenty-something dropouts who always come out on top. Wayne and his best friend Garth present a small cable show that has a huge following. An ambitious executive seizes the chance to make money out of them, and in doing so almost destroys their show. Meanwhile, the heroes' friendship is tested by Wayne's relationship with a rock singer. Everything is ultimately resolved, but not before audiences are given a sad end, followed by an alternative Scooby Doo finale. Along the way there is Carvey's impressive Cary Grant impression, a send-up of popular films and TV shows and the classic rendition of Queen's 'Bohemian Rhapsody' in a car. Wayne's utterly unlikely love interests are played by Tia Carrere and Lara Flynn Boyle, while Rob Lowe is suitably slimy as the double-dealing executive. With its puerile adolescent humour, *Wayne's World* is the perfect all-American family entertainment…*Not!*

INDEX

BIOGRAPHIES

Warren Elsmore is an artist in LEGO® bricks and lifelong fan of LEGO, based in Edinburgh, UK. He has been in love with the plastic brick since the age of four and is now heavily involved in the LEGO fan community. Since rediscovering his love of LEGO at the age of 24, Warren has never looked back. After 15 years in a successful IT career, he moved to working full time with LEGO bricks in 2012 and now helps many companies to realise their own dreams in plastic.

Warren's first two books, *Brick City* and *Brick Wonders*, were released worldwide to critical acclaim. Since their release, the models from both books have gone on tour in museums and galleries, attracting tens of thousands of visitors to every location. You can learn more about both Warren and his brick masterpieces at www.warrenelsmore.com.

Nick and Caroline Savage both grew up with LEGO. They rediscovered it in adulthood after suddenly realising they could buy it without asking their parents for permission. After having this epiphany, they founded Minifigs.me with a mission to create the world's best custom LEGO minifigures. Since then, they've created many thousands of minifigs, depicting everything from customers' families to high-profile celebrities for TV shows and the press. In 2013, they were joined by their first permanent member of staff – their baby daughter, Indiana. She'll no doubt have all the LEGOs she needs.

Teresa 'Kitty' Elsmore was a LEGO fan as a child and continues to enjoy creating models with LEGO bricks today. Her passion is for organic forms, such as the trees and gardens you see in this book. Since their marriage in 2005, Teresa and Warren have collaborated on a number of projects, and she is responsible for many of the intricate details in the minifig scenes.

Kirsten Bedigan is a classical archaeologist and ancient historian based in Edinburgh, UK. She was introduced to LEGO as a young child and has not stopped playing with it since.

PICTURE CREDITS